ON
ALLIUM AVENUE

BUGS IN THE BACKYARD

FRANK PREM

what
lies buried
deep
in the allium
flower . . .

Title: *On Allium Avenue* – Bugs in The Backyard
ISBN: 978-1-925963-78-6 (h-bk)
ISBN: 978-1-925963-77-9 (p-bk)
ISBN: 978-1-923166-42-4 (Fixed Format EPub)
ISBN: 978-1-923166-43-1 (PDF)

Published in 2025 by Wild Arancini Press

an allium (so beautiful)

who would have
thought
me
beautiful

who would think . . .

attractive

yes

I am

grateful (thank you)

thank you

why
thank you
so very much

I
don't mind
if I do

thank you

this way (for love)

this way

no
that way

I can't leave
though
I try

think
I've fallen
in love

a minute (fly)

I can
stay
a minute

only
just a minute . . .

to fly!

that's
the thing

slipping (oh!)

oh!

oh!

my . . .

my grip . . .

I think
I may be
losing . . .

my grip

oh dear

oh!

pretty (dull)

pretty
aren't I

it's dull here

look around . . .

dull
dull

thank heaven
for me

'scuse me (sorry)

sorry

sorry

'scuse my
bottom

there's just . . .

there's
something
I need

down

here

oh (sing it)

oh . . .

sing it with me

oh
I'm a handsome
guy
a
pretty
hover fly . . .

time (no, none)

can't stop
I
can't stop

I've got to go
got
to run

no time
now

no time

work (always work)

can anyone
stop work

just
for a minute . . .

oh

I forgot

you're ants

rosey (call me)

aha

this
is the life

these
are the heights

rosemary

call me
rosey

tumbler (in the flowers)

I
am a pintail

a jumper

come close
and I
will leap

a tumbler

busy (as . . .)

well . . .

it's summer

busy time

no-one can stop
working

not really

what lies within (the allium)

what
lies buried
deep
in the allium
flower . . .

only
the pollinators
know

one more drop (on the bottom)

there is
more . . .

another drop

there
it
is . . .

it's right
down
at the bottom

no time (never enough)

no no
haven't you
heard?

there's no time

there is never
quite enough
time

passing (mmm)

I don't
usually
dine here

but . . .

the allium aroma
is . . .

mmm

too beautiful (my wings)

I
will show
my wings
for you

mine
is the shade
that is
so
beautiful

mood (is blue)

am I
blue

I don't know . . .

maybe
it's
the mood I'm in

maybe . . .

nothing

just checking (catching rays)

I'm just
here
y'know

not doing much

catching rays

checking
the menu

here is (the buzz)

want to hear
the buzz . . .

lean in

listen

you ready . . .

    bzzzzzzz

d'ya get it?

    bzzzzzzz

ha ha

make way (we're busy)

'scuse me

coming through

'scuse me . . .

look

would you mind
moving

we're busy here

you have to be . . . (choosy)

oh
I don't visit
the alliums

no

they're
not *my* kind
of insect

so (tired)

sometimes
I get so . . .

so . . .

I get so
tired

I just need
to hide
away

the crooner (ba-ba-boo)

ba-ba-ba-boo . . .

hi babe

don't you know?

with looks
like mine

you have
to sing

time (in a while)

time . . .

I think

is
what you make it

I'll get moving
in
a little while

Extras, Out-takes (and Bloopers)

in (then out)

we were in
the story
at first

but
it just went
a different way

bottom's up (and tricky)

it was
a *trick*

he wanted
a close up

hee hee

he shot
my *bottom*!

movie (boo!) star

here's me
being
a movie star . . .

a dark-caped
scary
movie star

boo!

hop along (hop-along)

I don't even know
what's
going on

I was just –
sort of –
hopping past

mine (should have been)

I
should have been
the star

goodness knows
I'm handsome
enough
for the part

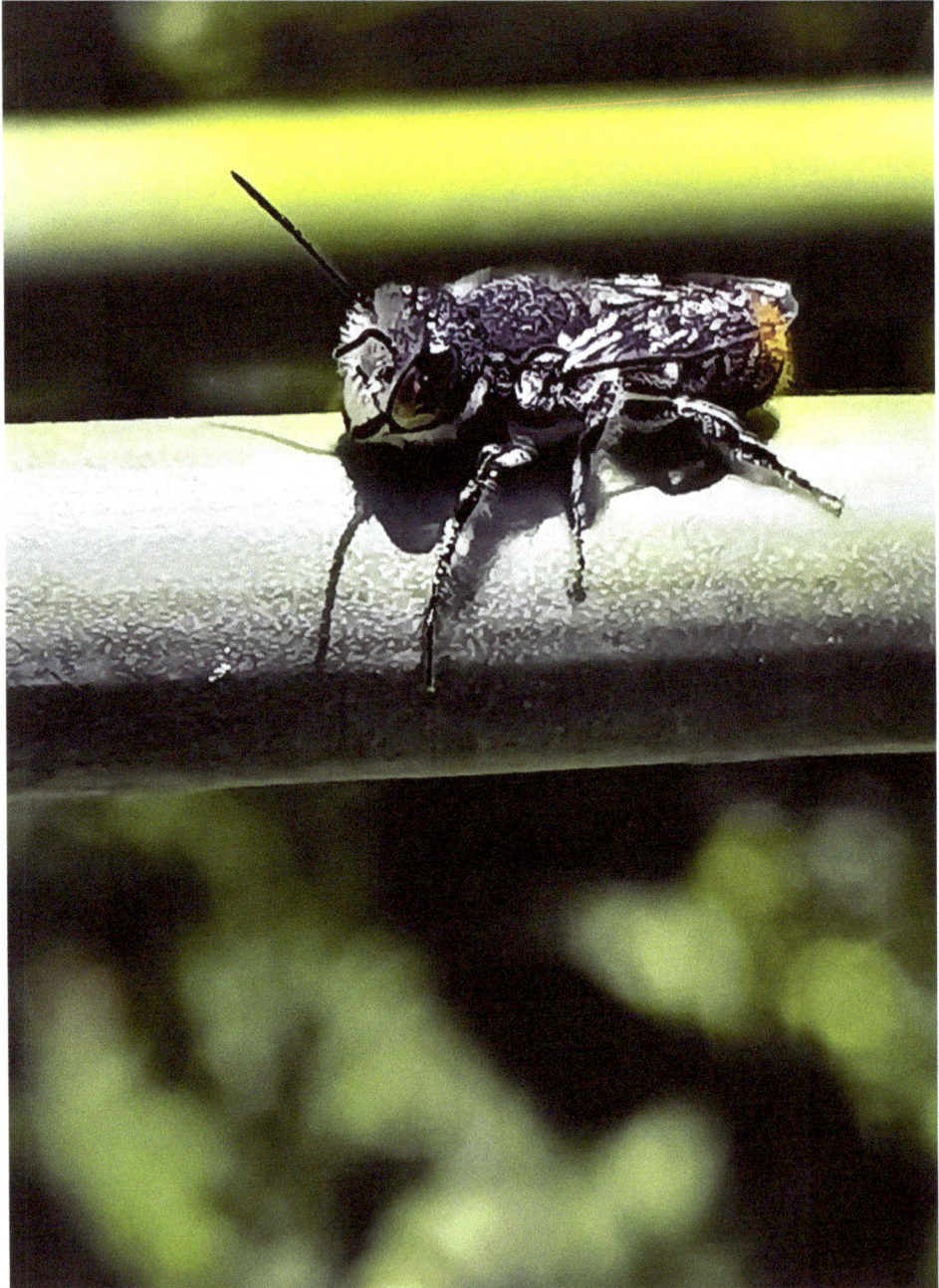

good night (it's been great)

it's *bee*-n
bee-utiful
to *bee*
with you

I'm tired now

so
good night

About Frank Prem

Frank Prem has been a storytelling poet since his teenage years. He has been a psychiatric nurse through all of his professional career, which now exceeds forty years.

He has been published in magazines, online zines, and anthologies in Australia, and in a number of other countries, and has both performed and recorded his work as spoken word.

He lives with his wife in the beautiful township of Beechworth in North East Victoria, Australia.

MORE BOOKS BY FRANK PREM

PICTURE POETRY BOOKS

THE BEECHWORTH BAKERY BEARS (2021)
VOICES (IN THE TRASH) (2021)
SHEEP ON THE SOMME (2021)

POETRY

SMALL TOWN KID (2018)
DEVIL IN THE WIND (2019)
THE NEW ASYLUM (2019)

HERJA, DEVASTATION — WITH CAGE DUNN (2019)

WALK AWAY SILVER HEART (2020)
A KISS FOR THE WORTHY (2020)
RESCUE AND REDEMPTION (2020)

PEBBLES TO POEMS (2020)

THE GARDEN BLACK (2022)
THE CIELONAUT (2022)

FrankPrem.com

www.ingramcontent.com/pod-product-compliance
Lightning Source LLC
Chambersburg PA
CBHW042347030426
42335CB00031B/3491